WALTER DEAN MYERS

A
TRIBUTE
FROM
THE HEART

We Are America

CHRISTOPHER MYERS

Collins
An Imprint of HarperCollinsPublishers

Collins is an imprint of HarperCollins Publishers.

We Are America: A Tribute from the Heart
Text copyright © 2011 by Walter Dean Myers
Illustrations copyright © 2011 by Christopher Myers
Manufactured in China.

Library of Congress Cataloging-in-Publication Data
Myers, Walter Dean, date
    We are America: a tribute from the heart / Walter Dean Myers ; Christopher Myers. — 1st ed.
        p.   cm.
    Summary: "A commemorative history of America and its people, told in free verse"—Provided by publisher
    ISBN 978-0-06-052308-4 (trade bdg.) — ISBN 978-0-06-052309-1 (lib. bdg.)
    1. United States—Juvenile poetry.   2. Children's poetry, American.   I. Myers, Christopher, ill.
II. Title.
PS3563.Y48T75   2011   2007011852
811'.54—dc22   CIP
                                                                                                                           AC

Typography by Martha Rago
11 12 13 14 15   SCP   10 9 8 7 6 5 4 3 2 1
❖
First Edition

"FOR AS MUCH OF YOU, CHRISTOPHER COLUMBUS, ARE GOING BY OUR COMMAND, WITH SOME OF OUR VESSELS AND MEN, TO DISCOVER AND SUBDUE SOME ISLANDS AND CONTINENT IN THE OCEAN . . ."

—*KING FERDINAND AND QUEEN ISABELLA*

AUTHOR'S NOTE

In the aftermath of the terror attacks on the World Trade Center, I witnessed first a collective grief, as people across the country mourned our losses, and then an outrage that the nation should be attacked. What came next was a spate of patriotism centered on defining, to a large extent, what it meant to be an American. Many of the definitions were bothersome, if for no other reason than that they didn't seem to include me. I was not given to waving flags and I studiously avoided the jingoism that followed 9/11. I was simply a person born and raised in the United States who took for granted the liberties and opportunities I found here. I wanted more from myself. It was no longer enough just to exercise my right to criticize both our history and our present state. I needed to take responsibility for that history, our present, and our future.

I began rereading the documents that formed the core ideas of what America is about—the Declaration of Independence, the Articles of Confederation, the Federalist Papers, and the Constitution—some of which I hadn't read since I was a teenager. I was reminded of the passion in which our country was created, a passion that would be universally inspirational and would be the model for governments all over the world.

We Are America comes from my heart, but it also comes from a lifetime of observations. I began the writing process by making myself learn more about my country, in order to understand why so many millions chose to come to our shores or, if they did not arrive by choice, how they still have prevailed. The writing has been a journey not of discovery but of rediscovery. No words here have been penned lightly, no flag waved mindlessly. This is simply my truest feelings for my country, my tribute to America.

—*Walter Dean Myers*

ARTIST'S NOTE

A steamboat creaks into the dock at Ellis Island. A young man reads faces and follows orders that he barely understands. His brother has told him that English is easy to understand; just like German but with a weird accent. But English is like English, and he doesn't understand anything, except that he is happy to be on land. A man in a uniform asks him a question, then again in perfect German: "Name?"

Mrs. Kloss is happy to have found her cleaning girl. She was surprised when that little slip of an Indian girl could speak the language. The girl says her mother is Pennsylvania Dutch and her father is an Indian.

You can't tell she has any Dutch by looking at her. But sometimes when she's making the beds, she sings, "Eiei, reie, riddieoo" and you can't hear a bit of Indian about her.

In the summer, working on the ice truck is one of the best jobs. Most of the time they ride on top of the ice bricks, waving to their sweaty, hot friends, whose work is selling vegetables or sweeping streets or whatever. One time when they get home, jingling with their tip money and chilled to the bone, Lee complains to Pap that he can't feel his fingers. Pap says, "You're lucky to have fingers. Once when I was a boy, I saw the master chop two fingers off a little girl for stealing." Lee doesn't complain to Pap again.

Mary has two uniforms and barely enough time to change between them. Mornings, wearing her apron and white cap, she heads to the Wrigley's factory and folds sticks of gum into paper foil. Then she changes into her black pants, and the red jacket with the gold buttons, for her job ushering at the movie theater. She sees every kind of movie, so many that she almost doesn't mind that she's too tired at the end of her days to dream. Her dreams are projected for her every afternoon.

What we know about him: He had a white horse (though not everybody had seen it) and he could read. In fact, he could recite poetry. He once recited Whitman's "O Captain! My Captain!" at one of those poetry recitals in Harlem that fancy Negroes liked to hold.

For the photo she poses in a bought dress she borrowed from her sister Eva. Mind you, the bought dress doesn't fit as well as the handmade dress her grandmother stitched. After all, her grandmother has been making dresses since she was a little girl at the Bower. But even her grandmother admits there's something sharp about a colored lass having her photograph taken in a newish store-bought dress. And you can see it in the picture.

Here are six people. All struggling, all discovering, all proving themselves. In Pennsylvania, in West Virginia, in New York, in Baltimore. All united in asking, whether or not they knew they were asking, "What can I make of my life?" "How will I define myself?" "What is America, and what will I make of it?"

Here are my grandparents, both adoptive and biological. None of them were rich or became rich. But they did leave me something special: They all left me their questions. "What is this place now? And what will this place be after I am gone?"

We Are America is one way I have of answering their questions, my dreams of what this rich country is, was, and will continue to be. This is my way of asking the questions, because in some way the beauty of this country is its open-endedness, the question mark of it. Where other places in the world end in periods, neat packets of sealed identities, we end in possibilities.

—*Christopher Myers*

Before there was America

Before the ships came

Their white sails ablaze

    against the clear blue sky

My Lakota heart pounded the rhythms

Of this sacred land

The warm spirit of the sun

    burned in my bosom

As my sons raced the wind

As my father sat in a curl of legend

As my grandmother

    stitched the giving earth

To the distant sky

A golden eagle, his wings spread like

    the Great Spirit's open arms

Flew over my people and the Comanche

    and the Iroquois

Its shadow passed Navajo and Hopi

It soared and soared

While sitting in the warm circle of my village

I dreamed

"THIS LAND BELONGS TO THE FIRST WHO SITS DOWN ON HIS BLANKET. . . ."

—*TECUMSEH*

"THIS IS THE PLACE WHERE THE LORD WILL CREATE A NEW HEAVEN AND A NEW EARTH."

—EDWARD JOHNSON

Before I knew that there was America

I had a freedom dream

The light and color of discovery lay just beyond

      the next wave, the next sunrise

I believed there was more than

      the trembling heart

      the careful peering into the darkness

      the promise of the rising tide

I dreamed a freedom dream

I heard a freedom song

The pull of hope

The taut bow of anticipation

The arrow of adventure

Flying across the ocean

I found an endless land

Its promise flowering in lush fields

Purple mountains etching their majesty in the pure air

Flat plains that absorbed the warm summer rains

Canyons that swallowed the imagination

And freedom

Freedom like water on the tongues of thirsting men

Freedom as sweet as young love

Before there was an America

I lit my fire at the mouth of the Congo
I watched a dark wisp of smoke
    cut a silver moon in half
    knowing it was a praise prayer
Before there was an America
I forged iron in Guinea and brass in Benin
Each morning I summoned the sun
    over the Ogun River

Each night I watched the sunset as it bled
    behind the mosques at Tombouctou
I found no freedom in this strange
    and beautiful land
But freedom lived
In my heart
Like an eagle
Longing to fly

We called ourselves Bostonians

New Yorkers, Georgians

Americans

We were the youth that could not fail

Planting our high ideals in virgin lands

      and eager hearts

Making vows forever brighter than

      the story we would live

Pledging an allegiance to liberty

And justice

That would forever mark us as a people

"THE QUESTION BEFORE THE COURT AND YOU GENTLEMEN OF THE JURY
IS NOT OF SMALL OR PRIVATE CONCERN; IT IS NOT THE CAUSE OF A POOR
PRINTER, NOR OF NEW YORK ALONE, WHICH YOU ARE NOW TRYING.
NO! . . . IT IS THE CAUSE OF LIBERTY."

—ANDREW HAMILTON

We raised up factories
and farms
great houses and small
Structures to challenge the pyramids
A free society busily creating a universe
      that only we could imagine
We defied the dazzled world
And still, and still
We wanted more
We wanted to be free of tyranny
Free from kings and queens
To pursue our own ideas
Our own destiny
No, we demanded it!

"Is life so dear, or peace so sweet, as to be purchased at
the price of chains and slavery? Forbid it, Almighty God!
I know not what course others may take; but as for me,
give me liberty, or give me death!"

—Patrick Henry

"WE HOLD THESE TRUTHS TO BE SELF-EVIDENT, THAT ALL MEN ARE CREATED EQUAL,
THAT THEY ARE ENDOWED BY THEIR CREATOR WITH CERTAIN UNALIENABLE RIGHTS,
THAT AMONG THESE ARE LIFE, LIBERTY, AND THE PURSUIT OF HAPPINESS."
—DECLARATION OF INDEPENDENCE

We were willing to die
to forge our dream

Knowing it was not enough to simply *be*

We needed to create ourselves

In the image of the new mind

Separated from our past, our history

Our poets, Jefferson, Madison, Franklin

Washington, Adams, Hamilton

Wrote the verses that made revolution irresistible

We danced a youthful dance

In a wild celebration of who we were

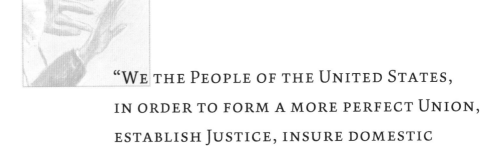

"WE THE PEOPLE OF THE UNITED STATES, IN ORDER TO FORM A MORE PERFECT UNION, ESTABLISH JUSTICE, INSURE DOMESTIC TRANQUILITY ..."
—CONSTITUTION OF THE UNITED STATES

"His Britannic Majesty acknowledges the said United States, viz. New Hampshire, Massachusetts Bay, Rhode Island and Providence Plantations, Connecticut, New York, New Jersey, Pennsylvania, Delaware, Maryland, Virginia, North Carolina, South Carolina and Georgia, to be free, sovereign and independent States."

—*King George III*

Like clumsy children
we fell

As we learned to run

Stumbled as we invented our own truths

We were America, but we were also

Thousands of souls smothering beneath the hatches

A chorus of chaos filling the air

     at Wounded Knee

The shocked stillness at Chapultepec Castle

Ambition betrayed us

Power was too strong a temptation

And yet, and yet . . .

We could hold up our sins for the world to see

Condemning our wrongs even as

     we committed them

We learned to light the darkness

     with the blazing torch that is

The Constitution

"IT MAY SEEM STRANGE THAT ANY MEN SHOULD DARE TO ASK A JUST GOD'S ASSISTANCE IN WRINGING THEIR BREAD FROM THE SWEAT OF OTHER MEN'S FACES."
—ABRAHAM LINCOLN

"WHAT, TO THE AMERICAN SLAVE, IS YOUR FOURTH
OF JULY? I ANSWER, A DAY THAT REVEALS TO HIM,
MORE THAN ALL OTHER DAYS IN THE YEAR, THE
GROSS INJUSTICE AND CRUELTY TO WHICH HE IS
THE CONSTANT VICTIM."

—FREDERICK DOUGLASS

We moved on stubbornly

Shedding our blood

      to prove who we were

That we were a high-minded people

Courageous

We died at Shiloh and Antietem Creek

      at Fort Wagner

We suffered at Gettysburg and Atlanta

Fell to the earth at Vicksburg
Cried out in the lonely night
        on Lookout Mountain
We emerged wounded and weary
But believing in the idea of a dream
That would be forever great
Proud to call that dream
America

"A HOUSE DIVIDED AGAINST ITSELF CANNOT STAND."
—ABRAHAM LINCOLN

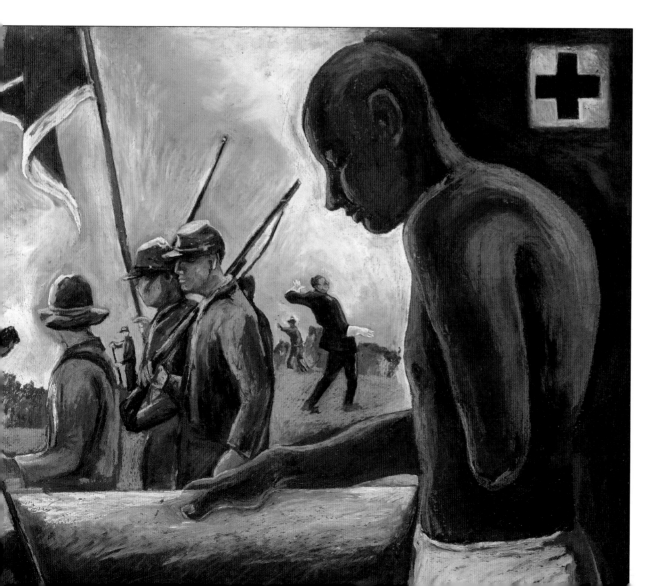

"GIVE ME YOUR TIRED, YOUR POOR,

YOUR HUDDLED MASSES YEARNING TO BREATHE FREE."

—EMMA LAZARUS

We were machines
belching smoke
Pushing carts, baking bricks, cleaning sewers
Inventing, daring, lifting our hopes to skies
      that suddenly seemed
Within reach
We were Irish muscle and Polish pride
Germans and Italians
Africans and Chinese
Mexican and English
We spoke a hundred languages
We were laborers building the hugeness
      the fantasy that was
The United States of America
We built silver rails stretching to the far horizon
Factories pounding out iron and steel
Cars, planes
Steamboats sailing down the Erie,
The Hudson, the Missouri, the Mississippi
Trolleys across the heart of Harlem

We were the flat gold plains
of Kansas
       feeding a hungry world
The snow-tipped Rocky Mountains
       scratching God's belly
The twisting route of the Chisholm Trail
The coverlet of bluebonnets along the
       Texas roadside
Bold and beautiful and breathtaking
America

We are America

The land of the free

Wealthy beyond belief

     and not wealthy

The land of equal opportunity

     and not equal

The land of justice

     and injustice

And from the tensions

From the struggle between conscience

And human frailty

Between the great hope of tomorrow

And the forever hunger of today

We have found our nation

"We have a positive vision of the future founded on the belief that the gap between the promise and reality of America can one day be finally closed."

—Barbara Jordan

To each child a freedom dream
To each soul the sweet taste of liberty
To each heart give the promise
Of America

QUOTATIONS

"For as much of you, Christopher Columbus, are going by our command, with some of our vessels and men, to discover and subdue some Islands and Continent in the ocean . . ."

—King Ferdinand and Queen Isabella of Spain, document addressed to Christopher Columbus, 1492

The technical development of the caravel, a smallish but agile ship, allowed for longer sea voyages. In 1492, Columbus took three caravels, the *Niña*, the *Pinta*, and the *Santa Maria*, to the Bahamas. This was not the first arrival of a European to the land that would one day be called America. But it introduced a major power to new lands.

"[This land] belongs to the first who sits down on his blanket or skins which he has thrown upon the ground; and till he leaves it no other has a right . . ."

—Tecumseh, a Shawnee chief, in a speech to Indiana Territory Governor William Henry Harrison, 1810

Native Americans continually lost their lands through treaties with white settlers, who regarded land as personal property from which they excluded others. Native Americans, called "Indians" by the Europeans, were eventually forced onto reservations.

" . . . this is the place where the Lord will create a new Heaven and a new Earth. . . ."

—Edward Johnson, a Puritan minister, 1654

For Puritans and other Europeans the new land was a place to experience freedom from religious or class bigotry.

"The question before the Court and you gentlemen of the jury is not of small private concern; it is not of the poor printer, nor of New York alone, which you are now trying. No! . . . It is the cause of liberty."

—Andrew Hamilton's defense of John Peter Zenger, 1735

Hamilton persuasively introduced the concept of a free press, a fundamental factor in defining American freedom, while defending Zenger, publisher of the *New York Weekly Journal*, against charges of libeling the British government.

"Is life so dear, or peace so sweet, as to be purchased at the price of chains and slavery? Forbid it, Almighty God! I know not what course others may take; but as for me, give me liberty, or give me death!"

—Patrick Henry, address to the Virginia Convention, 1775

American colonists felt that individual liberty should be extended far beyond what they had experienced under British rule. But how far would the colonists go? For Henry there could be no compromise.

"We hold these truths to be self-evident, that all men are created equal, that they are endowed by their Creator with certain unalienable Rights, that among these are Life, Liberty, and the pursuit of Happiness."

—The Declaration of Independence, July 1776

After a few major skirmishes with British soldiers, the thirteen colonies declared their independence in a proclamation espousing individual human rights. The British called it treason. The Revolutionary War began. The fighting would not end until 1781.

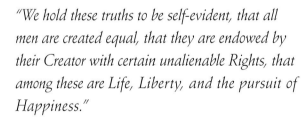

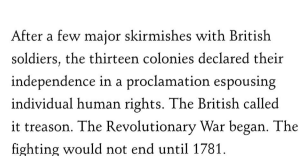

"We the People of the United States, in order to form a more perfect Union, establish Justice, insure domestic Tranquility . . .
—The Constitution of the United States, ratified 1787

How would the former colonies combine into one country? Could a small state like Rhode Island hold its own against a large and powerful state like Pennsylvania? How would the idea of liberty—one that Americans proclaimed so loudly—extend to the thousands of black slaves? It is this document, with its amendments, that is fundamental to our constitutional republic.

His Britannic Majesty acknowledges the said United States, viz. New Hampshire, Massachusetts Bay, Rhode Island and Providence Plantations, Connecticut, New York, New Jersey, Pennsylvania, Delaware, Maryland, Virginia, North Carolina, South Carolina and Georgia, to be free, sovereign and independent states. . . ."
—Treaty of Paris, ratified 1784

With limited resources and the help of French allies, the Americans defeated a better-trained British army in 1781. The Treaty of Paris formally severed ties between the United States and Great Britain.

"It may seem strange that any men should dare to ask a just God's assistance in wringing their bread from the sweat of other men's faces."
—Abraham Lincoln, second inaugural address, 1865

President Lincoln, like many Americans, questioned how people could reconcile slavery with Christian beliefs.

"What, to the American slave, is your Fourth of July? I answer, a day that reveals to him, more than

all other days in the year, the gross injustice and cruelty to which he is the constant victim."
—Frederick Douglass, speech to a crowd of slaves, 1852

Douglass's speech reflected a tenet of the American system of beliefs: the freedom and willingness to be open to self-criticism.

"A house divided against itself cannot stand."
—Abraham Lincoln's acceptance of his nomination to the U.S. Senate by the Illinois Republican Party, 1858

Lincoln did not believe one nation could exist "half slave, half free." By 1858 the rift between the agricultural South, whose economic system relied on slavery, and the industrial North had grown so great that Southern states wanted to secede from the Union.

"Give me your tired, your poor, Your huddled masses yearning to breathe free."
—Emma Lazarus, "The New Colossus," 1883

In Lazarus's poem America embraces its immigrants. However, restrictions on immigration, such as the Chinese Exclusion Acts, suggest that the dream of America was brighter than the reality.

"We have a positive vision of the future founded on the belief that the gap between the promise and reality of America can one day be finally closed."
—Barbara Jordan, Democratic National Convention, 1976

During America's bicentennial year, Jordan, a Texas member of the House of Representatives, reminded us of our freedom dream.

ART NOTES

pp 8–9: Lakota scout; ghost dance; New York City; Will Rogers

pp 10–11: John Smith; refugee boat

pp 12–13: Duke Kahanamoku; Amelia Earhart

pp 14–15: Ironworkers, Benin; university, Tombouctou; Dr. Mae Jemison

pp 18–19: Shuggie Otis; Dave Brubeck; Transamerica Building, San Francisco; John Hancock Building, Chicago; textile mill, Lowell, Massachusetts

pp 22–23: Battle of Wounded Knee; Big Foot, Sioux chief; Japanese internment camp

pp 24–25: Civil War; World War I; World War II; Vietnam; Iraq War

pp 26–27: Brick maker; Chinese railroad workers; Lower East Side, New York City; Detroit

pp 28–29: Mark Twain; Mississippi River

pp 30–31: From left to right, top row: Gloria Steinem; Albert Einstein; Yuri Kochiyama; Fiorello La Guardia; Hedy Lamarr; Richard Feynmann; Max Baer; bottom row: Cesar Chavez; Thomas Alva Edison; I. M. Pei; Jean-Michel Basquiat; Anna May Wong: all first-generation Americans or naturalized citizens

pp 32–33: Jimi Hendrix

pp 34–35: From left to right, top row: Greg Louganis; Danny Thomas; Malcolm X; Dolores Huerta; Abraham Lincoln; Gertrude Stein; Jack Johnson; William Carlos Williams; Thomas Jefferson; James Baldwin; 2nd row: Katherine Dunham; Daniel Inouye; Martha Graham; Annie Sullivan; Helen Keller; Maria Tallchief; 3rd row: Frederick Douglass; George Gershwin; Buster Keaton; Zora Neale Hurston; Martin Luther King, Jr.; Kalpana Chawla; Franklin Delano Roosevelt